DIANE WAKOSKI

CAP OF DARKNESS.

Including

Looking for the King of Spain
&
Pachelbel's Canon

BLACK SPARROW PRESS
Santa Barbara - 1980

CAP OF DARKNESS: INCLUDING "LOOKING FOR THE KING OF SPAIN" & "PACHELBEL'S CANON."
Copyright © 1980 by Diane Wakoski.

Thanks to the editor of The Atlantic Review where "Pamela's Green Tomato Pie" originally appeared.

LIBRARY OF CONGRESS CATALOGING IN PUBLICATION DATA

Wakoski, Diane.
    Cap of darkness.

    I. Title.
PS3573.A42C3   811'.54   80-149
ISBN 0-87685-454-4
ISBN 0-87685-453-6 pbk.
ISBN 0-87685-455-2 signed cloth ed.

TO THE MEMORY OF ROBINSON JEFFERS

TABLE OF CONTENTS

Cap of Darkness

Preface

Preface

23 October 1972

DEAR MICHAEL,

Like Egypt and the Sphinx, you have been part of my fantasy life for the past two years. I suppose all that means—and I do not really know why I should tell you or anyone this, since the beauty of our fantasy lives is that no one can take them away, they being totally private, and even poets have fantasies they do not share with anyone . . .

all that means is that I must have met you at a time, and in a place when I needed an image, an idea to cling to, in order to live with some difficult reality, and that you must have had the right mustache or voice, read the right poem, or touched me in some special way.

The most real connections I have in my life right now, and perhaps that is an ideal, are by letter. I think I'm looking for something different from anything I ever wanted before, and letters have become more real than any of the people I know. I have discovered too, that all poems are letters, and

nothing is simple or innocent anymore. Except poetry.

Memories: Fantasies

lovers
do not love,
> tho I suppose travellers travel
> and losers lose.
I am only a traveller because there are places I need to go;
and when I met Michael
I loved another man
whom it was impossible to love.
He rode his motorcycle
on a dirt track I called

Allegory.
It was in my living room,
and my own name was Moon,
One Who Finishes Far Behind In The Race,
but I owe him everything,
even the memory of the ocean full of cascading fish,
their silver bones like keys in my pocket,
their shining skins gleaming on my arms as I rode
through the night
behind Motorcycle Rider,
with a helmet of broken promises, dripping down on my
shoulder
as trout and smelt and wiggling sardines.

When I met Michael,
he was a surprise,
like finding a silver snake in your bed and not being
quite sure if you did like snakes;
he was a mustache
and a pair of shoulders,
an image
like the moon
        to remember on a dark night.

                Do you remember Michael?
                I said to a nameless hiker
                on another dirt track?
                    Yes, he kissed
              you.

No, I say,
you are thinking of someone else;
a motorcyclist who lives in the New England woods.

Ramble.
I ramble on this dirt track. Not called Allegory
anymore
since I am trying to remember Michael,
a man I made up in my head,

my brother,
who jumped off a cliff into a California ocean,
too young for a mustache, memories, or
poetry.

Lovers do not love.
Or they find that love is something to fear,
something to run away from,
a snake under a bare foot,
a silver trap which catches a moment of light from the moon,
just as the paw of the mountain lion
passes near it;

if lovers do not love,
perhaps the losers
do not lose
either.
Is there any way to lose,
when there is certainly no way to possess?

In my mind,
I own you
hoard you,
save you up,
do not let anyone know
what amount of you
I have.
Do not let anyone know
that what they think I have lost
is really only the head of the sardine; I have
in my mind
memories
of a whole,
   leaping,
     shining like a keyring,
        silver as a thumbtack,
uninvented
fish.

WHISTLING

Walking out to my car
the shadows of the parking lot
like sleeping alligators
are matter-of-fact
realities.

Whistling.
I hear someone whistling
behind the brick wall to the garden.
He is not walking; the
sound comes from one place,
like an owl that sits in the same old tree
each night.
I remember someone who whistles
who is not here,
will not ever be here.

The scar on my knee
which was a wound when I was six;
the light streak on
my small Persian rug
where once a table stood in the sunshine
for many years;
my memory
which has a needle in it
surrounded by new flesh/ glows hot
from that whistling
in the dark.
I have learned to love
Southern accents,
sounds from the
shadows.
The missing man.
The King of Spain.

16

TELLING YOU TRUE, ABOUT MY FANTASY LIFE

For M. W.

Wdnt let anybody
really know
what I think when I turn out the lights
at bedtime.

Or sit in airports
waiting
for planes.
            How I turn you into the
racing car driver
who will pick me up at the other airport when my plane
lands,
        or see you
as the man with the black mustache
and heavy tweed coat
walking up the ramp, American or United,
with an expensive camera
and a copy of *The Wall Street Journal*;
who smiles at me
when I drop my copy of *Road and Track*,

or how I close my eyes and pretend that I am lying on a beach
with a gorgeous tan that makes the scars
which show above my yellow bikini
gleam
        and look exotic
rather than ugly,
and that you are with me and we are making love,
tho never in my life have I been on a beach
where it was private enough
to make love
                yes,
                that's fantasy for you,

it would be boring,
no doubt,
for you to know that
I have often pretended some man I was with
was you
        so that I could talk more
engagingly,
so that I could be interested in him at all;
or if he were so hopeless that I could not imagine
his ever being you,
then I would pretend that you were standing on the
other side
of the room,
watching me as I talked to him,
until my face became animated and the things I said
were like dreams or poems
and you, the unseen audience, with your cynical smile
and diffident manner,
would let me know you were watching,
tho you'd never say anything,
and I would walk past you, on the way out of the room,
going I suppose with the boring fellow to dinner,
or to sit in a bar,
and smile at you and wonder what you thot, as you nodded,
diffidently,
again,
    ironically,
        actually,
           and then I would realize
that even the imaginary you
which I invented
who was not even standing there
had also disappeared,
as I walked out of the room,
and that now I missed my own invention,
as much as I originally missed you,
              the source
of my invention.

Oh, and you would never believe
the physique I invented for you, though I can scarcely remember
if you are tall or short,
broad-shouldered or thin,
and the fact that when I dream of fucking
you are often the man doing it,
though I have never met a man, any King of Spain, who liked
to fuck as much as I do
                    all women, according to a good poet I know
                    are nymphomaniacs
                    when they get a chance
but since I live with you only in my
imagination, I am privileged to invent you as someone
meeting my specifications.
My imaginary scenes with you are always arrivals and departures.

The man I love
must simultaneously show his love for me
and be cool about it,
but the part I always get best, in my fantasies
is the being cool part,
and even in my imagination, you often walk away
with some other girl,
or alone,
or have not been wanting to touch me
as I wanted to be touched.

This explanation is addressed to:
                    The King of Spain
                    My Motorcycle Betrayer
                    The Woodsman
                    The Astronomer
                    A Poet
                    A Truck Driver
                    A Mountain Climber
and you,
who have no name,

and fit the silhouette of all the above,
putting your arms around me when I am cold,
so that I smell the tobacco smoke in your clothes
and feel assured that a man might take care of me,
                                        someday.

My body is ugly.
My face, not beautiful.
My conversation topical and limited.
Sometimes I try to believe in my imagination,
but when I reveal it,
the poor rag reads like *Esquire* or *Playboy*
or worse,
The Ladies' Home Journal.
And yet I still believe in the tree which made the pulp
for all this poor paper.
Don't pity me.
I am proud proud proud.
And honest.
Honest,
like a dormant volcano
you've trusted
too long.

DISCOVERING MICHAEL AS THE KING OF SPAIN

There is a photograph
someone has taken of us,
                        Michael,
we are facing each other,
in fencing tunics—grey with red hearts over the left breast
(indicating something pulses underneath)
our foils are crossed, the tips resting pointed against the heart.

Poised in time and space,
two lovers who in the photo do not love
but are on the verge of piercing each other's hearts,
a scene from a tarot deck,
or a Cocteau movie.
Photos live
because they are moments which cannot be destroyed.
Museum moments,
not satisfying, but lasting.
        Explanation:
        why I love the King of Spain:
because no one knows who he is.
A photo perhaps?
Or museum moment
in my eye?

He cannot be destroyed or taken away.
Cannot leave me.

Today,
I was tempted to speak to you
to tell you
that you were
my King of Spain,
but saw again that photo
so accurately taken,

you and I,
in our grey tunics,
foils pointed at each other's red patch hearts,
frozen in our fascination for each other's fantasies,
respecting life when so close to death . . .

If you are the King of Spain,
then the King of Spain was never mine.
The King of Spain will always
be there,
to walk with
              at dawn on the beach,
or to leave his footprints
                  for me to see.
When you, and all other men,
have deserted me for more beautiful women
or more talented and charming ones,
I will still meet the King of Spain
privately.

I wanted you to be
the King of Spain
             today,
because I have felt
so deserted.
Instead, I told you boldly
like a full moon coming out before dark in its assurance,
feeling as frightened and foolish, tho,
                  as some Southern honeysuckle vine,
I said
I loved you,
knowing you,
not the King of Spain,
could be destroyed, taken away,
that you could leave me,
love being weak and powerless, perhaps even ephemeral.

But knowing,
to call you the King of Spain
would be cowardly
would make you disappear into my head,
an invisible mysterious lover no one could ever take away,
but one who also could not touch me every/any day.

I chose dangerous life
over safe poetry, this time,
knowing that my muse, for once,
was smiling and nodding
                    seeing
her favorite daughter for one human moment as woman,
not dangerous metaphor.

The moment after
the photo was taken,
moving now,
one red patch pierced with the steady tip
of thin steel.

TOUCHING THE KING OF SPAIN UNDER WATER

He was a coral reef
and I the barrier,
a divided concept, words
that work against
each
other.
        I once thought
of water
as time or space;
that it supported and suspended
the fans
of moving creatures
great banks of snails drifting towards
rays of light–
colored angel fish,
the dark clack of morays like dead leaves on the ground
hidden under the alien bare foot, I dreamed
water was
touching my lips when I was thirsty
but could only know
that time and space and water
aside
you were there once and touched me,
like water,
and are not there now
to touch me;
all those concepts
are vanished,
water evaporated on a
hot day,
or dammed up
on the other side of

24

some big mountain range/
                    he was a coral reef,
I, the barrier.

Poetry,
some ocean.

IN PRAISE OF MODERN TIMES

She formed bowls
in her hands
as soft and vibrating as the throat
of a bullfrog hidden in the marsh,
his deep voice booming
like large clay pots,
terra cotta saucers catching
the water
that seeped down through
captured earth;

she was
a potter,
earth's
servant.
He was a prince. The King of Spain.
I found many fairy tales
in which they lived happily
ever after.

But no story impressed me
as much
as dipping my hands into the cool brook
and picking up the frog/ it was the length
of my little finger,
a miniature
with a voice like the cracking
of a cup on a hot stove,
soft and moist,
he stretched his throat and I let him
hop
back into the water.

Pleasure and pain are physical.

Beauty is fact.
There is no lost love.
None found,
for that matter,
either.

Cap of Darkness

SPENDING THE NEW YEAR WITH THE MAN
FROM RECEIVING AT SEARS

We have dismissed,
like a doorbell being rung by someone who
has forgotten his key to the building,
my childhood.
My mother:
a bookkeeper who secretly loved women
from her well of loneliness.
My father:
the sea captain figure,
whose bedroom never contained Lafcadio Hearn's
Glimpses of Unfamiliar Japan
waterspotted from the Yangtze River.
My sister who married a lineman with the phone company,
a man who hang glides like a giant eagle over the Pacific.
And I, who probably should have died in a teenage accident:
first childbirth, when a drunken doctor cut me nearly in two and I
bled
for three weeks.

But instead, here I am,
like everyone else,
scarred,
clinging to the rubber raft at my fortieth birthday,
thinking of my son who is twenty-one and whom I have not seen for
twenty-one years.
I have mourned and mourned
the loss of Rilke's mustache,
not that he lost it,
but that he left me,
wearing it,
I, never to see it, like my son, again.

It is hard to imagine women
not wearing black shawls down to their ankles,
standing on cliffs over the desert,
or the ocean,
wailing,
singing for their men, lost at sea, gone to war,
or simply away,
having walked out of those black shawled lives;
yet women are the ones who wear bright colors,
paint their faces into masks,
and wear diamonds and sapphires,
even if they do not own them.
And today, hide the shawls
in a cookie jar the shape of a penguin
on a kitchen counter.

*   *   *

Scene:
though dismissed.

Not quite dismissed.

I remember it,
my mother and sister and I sitting on the sagging couch in our house
in the orange grove,
the couch with the spring sticking out
on which I gouged my knee and began the bleeding which was never
to stop.
The new Sears Roebuck catalogue had come.
I hated the clothes from Sears,
 but my mother loved the act of reading the book with us,
                    looking,
and asking us which things we would like to wear.
I learned that if it was in a book,
you could possess it.
                    (Those beautiful colors tumbling before my
                    eyes in the department store, you could not have.)

And when the packages arrived from Sears,
flat and often torn,
the clothing in them was drab,
the clothes squashed into flat wrinkled shapes.
And nothing which came from the catalogue looked like
its picture,
that picture which itself never looked as good
as the yellows and greens and burgundies
on the racks and shelves of Whittier, California's tiny department stores.
Those, you could not have.
You *could* have: Sears' (E) gingham dress, in sizes 2,4,6, and 6x.
                    Colors: blue or red.

Every year I wrote a letter to Santa Claus.
Dear Santa,
Please do not make me wear any more clothes from Sears. I know it is
                    the most
expensive, but could you bring me a dress and a sweater from Myers
                    Department Store
In Whittier, California?

*   *   *

I met you in Spain.
You were tall and (I thought) self-assured.

*   *   *

Years later a letter comes from you.
Are you still tall?
You must be self-assured. There are no typing mistakes
in your letter.

*   *   *

A Dissertation on Smallness

For some incredible reason
smallness is a kind of virtue in women
So, I grew up rather smug about my small body—
        five foot two,
          twenty-four inch waist, size five-and-a-half shoe.

Yet, there was also something wrong.
I knew it, but couldn't quite figure it out. Like my
mother
loving the Sears catalogue so much,
when I could plainly see
it contained ugly things.
Around the people I most admired,
I felt large and clumsy.
Now I understand that a little.
I loved them because they were smart or strong or
very good at something.
They made me want to grow. But growing,
growing . . .
        That was something which made you bigger.
And I had learned to think:

GOOD = SMALL

I was appalled at twenty-one when I found that I had grown an inch
      taller.
I was five foot three.
And a few years ago at my physical, I found that now
I am almost five four.

I found it amusing that people always thought
from pictures,
or seeing me on platforms,

that I was tall.
And upon being introduced to me, they would of course exclaim,
"But you're so little. I thought you would be tall."
I knew the guilty secret:
that I was almost five foot four, but smugly would say,
"No, I'm exactly five three.
Just the height of the average American woman."
Taking such comfort in the smallness.
The goodness.

By thirty, I wore a size six shoe.
At thirty-five, a six-and-a-half.
Today when I bought a pair of moccasins, I had to get a seven. And
when I look down
at my feet, I am horrified. They look big and ugly. And most of all,
they do not look
like my feet. My little feet.

I am telling myself all these things
in order to try to understand why I thought small was beautiful.
Womanly.
Desirable.
In retrospect, I see only a small smug
person,
hating the flat ugly packages arriving from Sears.
One who has failed at being a woman, rejecting motherhood,
failing wifehood,
and never succeeding as *femme fatale*.

*   *   *

Some women were discussing clothes and weight in my living room
last year. One witty woman said, "The size of dress you wear de-
pends on your wealth. If you buy a $100 dress, you may take only a
size seven. But if you buy a $15 dress, you may require a twelve. The
rich like to think of themselves as small."

And a famous *bon mot* of our times: "You can never be too thin or too rich."

My eyes see things diminished, though. I bought two Pendleton shirts for friends at Christmas last year, and both men were insulted because the shirts were several sizes too small. I guess everything tiny looks good to me. I want things to be beautiful. And beautiful
is,
no,
was once/ has always been,
small.

* * *

In Spain his silence seemed beautiful.
I felt beautiful.
Small in his big silences.

* * *

Looking for the King of Spain while reading Lorca,
Stevens, and Yeats,
and dreaming of Rilke's mustache.

* * *

Your silence is heavy like cigarette smoke,
and the smoke blows over into the New Year.

* * *

Carrying Rocks for My Garden

I am sitting
heavy and tired from my own heaviness.
I dismiss these things
but carry them with me.

We are on a boat which is docked on Lake Michigan.
I am no longer small,
but I have tried to make myself as small as possible,
and thus I am always cramped and hunched into my life, and feel tired
     and swollen
from small places.
The New Year is out there, large and empty, and I want to be big and
     walk
around in a space as big as Madison Square Garden.
No. As big as the Sahara Desert.
No. As much room as exists between the stars in the Milky Way.
But I am sitting tired and slumped in a big boat.

You are not the King of Spain,
but his crippled brother. You are tall but not as tall as he.
Your feet are bigger though, and while my own large feet appall me
I love your big feet.
I once put my (then) size six foot into Robert Kelly's size thirteen
     shoe.
He said, "That is obscene, Diane."
Yet, he has always known the value of largeness.
I have known it for men. I want my men to be bigger, smarter,
     stronger, richer
and more powerful than any other men in the world. I want them
     so big
they can carry me out of burning houses, so big they can hold me
against bad weather. But I wanted to be small.
Small.
To be protected.
To be small enough to be protected.
I wanted to be small to their bigness.
I needed to be small *because men are small too*, and I needed to be
smaller,
to be protected.
But my eyes which bought those shirts too small, diminish things.

A ray of light, hitting a certain optic nerve can change

the relative dimension
of objects being observed through that phenomenon.

You, walking in the rain,
along the beach of Lake Michigan,
gathering 25 pounds of rocks for my plants,
carrying them to me in a broken box.
You, the kind crippled brother of the King of Spain.

*   *   *

A friend saying to me
(another woman without a man)
"Where did you get him? He's so cute." Do grown
women still talk
like this?
Yes, we do.

"I got him from the Sears and Roebuck Catalogue."
She goes home to read her Sears catalogue.
One of my students found her man in the Eddie Bauer catalogue.
A far better selection, I should think,
but history is with me. You came from Sears. Memories
of my sad, dismissed
childhood, reading the Sears catalogue with my mother.
On my bed, there is a down comforter from Eddie
Bauer's.

Yes, it is hard to imagine women
not wearing black shawls down to their ankles.
I recently noticed, however, that the Sears catalogue
did not contain a single
shawl.

So now, I am thinking of the bigger bed,
the King Size (May I have one bed, King of Spain size,
please?)

for the big New Year
on which I will put my Eddie Bauer King Size down
comforter,
and we will sleep under it together.
You have quit your job in receiving at Sears,
and now we will each give and receive big things,
as I want to be able to give my son whom I have never seen
a big spirit.
I want my big feet to look beautiful to me.
I want to stand up to my full five foot four.
I guess there was something that was always too big and a little
		embarrassing
in me, bursting out of its seams,
constantly needing new shoes.

I want to claim it now,
and pass it on to my son and to my daughter,
and to share it with the Man from Receiving at Sears,
the crippled brother of the King of Spain,
the man who, still, loves me the most.

HAVING REPLACED LOVE WITH FOOD & DRINK

a poem for those who've reached 40

Sweet basil,
sturdy as my legs, aromatic from Donna's garden, its healthy
green leaves pungent
in a fist-sized bouquet on my kitchen sink.

Whirling
the leaves which I have snipped off
as carefully as buttons
in the sharp blades of La Machine,
adding both white fleshes of pine nut and garlic,
a long golden drink of sweet olive oil . . .

A-1 pesto
though I haven't used either mortar or pestle.

My linguini simmers.

This evening alone
with my books
handsome jungle of plants,
real clay:
       Pewabic,
       Grueby,
       Owens,
       Rookwood,
on my shelves.

Yes, I have gladly given up love
for all the objects made with love:
       a poem,
       an orchid,
       this pasta, green and garlicky
       made with my own hands.

PRECISION

Walking, remembering,

In the grass, I see what I think is
a small *coprinus*,
but I look more closely and decide:
        broken soda cracker.
Of course,
        this Southern California lawn
probably wouldn't be growing mushrooms.

I have already catalogued
Icelandic poppies—flamingo, salmon, vermillion,
party dresses—on the lawn,
and purple flags on another,
a whole bed of tiny white irises
and nasturtiums spilling over the cement-banked edge
of another yard.

It is March, and camellias are crowding
the bushes at every house,
pink, white, deep rose frills,
china-like,
        perfect.

Behind me, the mockingbird is singing one of his best songs,
        piccolo
        oboe
        harp
        and squeeking door all combined.
The drama is only a memory;
I arrived yesterday at the Los Angeles airport
and could not help some part of me wishing/expecting to see you,
M.,

waiting for me to return.
I suppose that is what it means
to be haunted.
In my real life
I neither expect
nor want you. Yet, some rehearsal of the past
is always with me.
Even this morning,
walking before breakfast in Santa Barbara
when I saw an ugly ranch house
with the porch light still on,
presumably from the night before,
I thought, "He hasn't come home. She is asleep
on the couch
with her clothes on, exhausted from
waiting most of the night."
And when I walked past another house
with the shades still drawn
but rock music pouring out of the closed windows, so incongru-
ously
at 8 a.m.
thought
of a young couple who have just
awakened to make love and don't want to do it
without the right music.
And I felt safe outside in the sunshine, just observing the flowers.
There is no way I can imagine
love, sex or romance
without pain,
the cutting, cutting
sharp knife of denials;
what I want now is an orderly world
where morning is
each beautful object in place,
the sun pouring in the window like champagne,
the china-white egg cup
with its neat boiled egg,

a burst of tulips, or poppies or
camellias on the table
                    in crystal
or cut glass,
the hot teapot, scalded and then filled with a fine dark tea,
and the day stretching plain,
unadorned
                    before me,
Mozart as companion,
a book,
a book,
about death
or life
but not about love.

We must go beyond beauty
to find it.
Invisible,
I want to wait for it
wearing the cap of darkness.

PAMELA'S GREEN TOMATO PIE

She stands by the sink
her feet neat and white,
her slim arms rolling the pie crust
and deftly arranging it in the pan so that
she can fill the cavity with
paper-thin
sliced
green tomatoes.

I am sitting in the carpeted room beyond the sink,
sipping a glass of burgundy,
talking to her husband, and watching her
as she clicks through the action,
glancing occasionally at the thick volume of *Gourmet*
then sprinkling brown sugar onto the swirl of tomato slices,
glancing again at the cookbook, continuing to
make small motions from which my attention wanders,
finally fitting the top crust on, with precision,
neatly made, a package compact and delectable, to be placed in the
        oven.

The woman who is making the green tomato pie
is a strange woman. She speaks English as if it were a foreign lan-
        guage to her,
but we all know it is not.
It sometimes makes me feel as if she is from another planet,
or a robot or android, programmed to be the perfect woman,
so beautiful and graceful,
intelligent and talented,
yet somehow,
none of those things quite meshing.
Unlike many beautiful women, she
does not make you gasp when

you see her slender body, clear eyes, blond hair
appear.
        Nor do her talents seem very extraordinary when you are
            faced with her life;
she is the kind of good dancer who makes a perfect partner, but
            whom no one notices,
perhaps for her very grace,
when she dances.

I sit there sipping my burgundy, asking myself
what the puzzle of this woman is,
that she should be special in so many ways,
yet nothing quite fits together,
none of it adds up to "extraordinary human being,"something we
            all call her husband
whose talents when separately enumerated
do not sound like so many as hers.

And she is a troubling friend to have;
she is so unhappy, and does not seem ever to fit properly into any
            life.
Yet, all that grace. And in spite of it,
I find myself often quarrelling with her, or preaching.
She leaves me so exasperated.

Like a button, just too large for the hole, the only one you could find
to sew on yr blouse which makes the whole front look lumpy but
which was the only button in the house even close to the size you
needed, and you couldn't go to work without sewing it on unless you
chose to use a safety pin.
She doesn't quite fit.

Yet, when she serves the green tomato pie,
its unusual flavor and delicate textures make even the non-pie eaters
            at the table
—like me—
murmur with appreciation and pleasure.

Her ten-year-old son eats two helpings. And he's a good kid, but
      not
really
a child gourmet.
So, here was something perfect she did,
her husband usually being the cook,
and it seemed exquisite,
like all of her life should be.
Yet no one remembered to tell her how exceptional it was when we
      left that evening,
though cooks in our crowd are always praised
for their special efforts.

It should have changed her image.
She should have become
the perfectly carved bone button, matching all the others
on the blouse.
But
even in my mind
she has not.
Even in retrospect, I think of the green tomato pie
as something not quite fitting in,
though it was so exceptional, it should not have been required to.

The pie was a perfect, almost unnoticed, moment in her life,
and I do not know why,
but she will not have many.

RED RUNNER

She comes at me in red tights
showing satin skin underneath,
and red shorts,
a red runner's jacket,

like a bird I don't expect to see
in the rain.

Thinking of fires I have built
and how flames are not
gratuitous,
how hard it is to get even
combustible material
                        to burn,
I wonder
how
she burns
through the continuous rain

(of Juneau),
this runner, young woman,
product of the 20th century.

When I passed her,
we exchanged a rather frank
brutal
glance.

She saw
a middle-aged woman,
bundled in a coat,
walking fast on her short legs.
Probably, to this red runner,

I appeared to be some slow
sea creature,
crawling along the bottom
of the ocean.

She ran past me,
like firecrackers
(which frightened me in my youth)
or sequins glittering on a dancer's costume,
a bottle of Tabasco which had put on an Adidas,
and, irrelevantly, I think of
a Carmen Miranda movie.

But this rain has come to mean
that things don't change.
When you reach a certain age, even the flame of a red satin–shorted
        runner,
coming like a can-can girl
out of the silver twilight
was not so much a change, as a proof of sameness.
Red runner,
reminder that I live
if not
in another time,
another world,
one where a flame is not easy
to coax into life,
one where I am outdated,
or extinguished,
or under water;
certainly no location for a flame.

RED RUNNER, AGAIN

Tonight
with a blue sweater
her red jacket tied around her waist
red shorts again,
this time her legs naked and
white as sea scallops.

She frowned
as she passed me again.
Scorpion fish,
sea slug,
slow mover in the silvery twilight.

NOT BREAKING THE SILENCE

In the shaping
great Yeats' head came through
all bloody, and allowing everyone to make his own judgment.

I live in the gulf between Beggar's Chili
and an evening beginning with *pâté de foie gras*,
neither loud enough nor restrained enough

remembering the words Medea spoke as she died in her chariot:

Where could I find love when I was no longer looking for love?

Laura, wearing her Mennonite cap, white bonnet of chastity,
       "If you untie the strings, the devil will pull it off "
spoke of the liberation provided by a wall of books.

Does she know she can be walled up behind those books,
just as Poe's hero was behind bottles of sherry?

When the time comes for the black man to walk in your door
with his big garden shears and you look out the window
to see if there is a buggy
or perhaps a chariot there

when you look out the window and see only your neighbor's
station wagon
then lock your doors.

Silence is the lock.
And finally, after all these years,
there are no keys.

SILVER

How much I want to sit down
at my table and pick up a heavy silver spoon to eat my soup. Why
do I want heavy sterling silver forks, knives, spoons, serving uten-
       sils? Why
do I want to put metal in my mouth?

Ask the wrong questions and you
will only get fools' answers.
Of course I do not want to put metal—even beautiful metal—in my
       mouth.
What I want
is to hold it and to somehow transform the ritual of eating
into something non-organic,
beyond the body,
beyond shit,
beyond decay,
beyond death. Of course
I want beautiful silver so that I can pretend I will never have to die.

AGING

It is the light
in January, thin as a beautiful woman's stocking
which I love.
It comes through my yellow curtains
in the morning
like clean underwear
and I,
warm and lazy under the down comforter
can only wonder
why there is such a general rejection of winter.

I'm not talking now
about freezing, starving soldiers
in the snow at Valley Forge;
but the simplicity of suburban snow
that is experienced by an ordinary
man or woman
in East Lansing, Michigan.

This winter
is so beautiful to me.

WHITE

To Norman Hindley

From a world of wet brown things,
I stepped into frozen winter;
clear ice slipcased the mountain ash
with their cherry-bunch clusters of berries,
and Jackie reminded me of
the Twelve Dancing Princesses, who wore out their silk shoes
each night
pirouetting in a castle
whose garden contained
winter–bare trees with branches holding rubies
and diamonds.
                    And Jackie gestured
with her delicate Southern fingers to illustrate
how
one could break off
a jeweled branch
at will.

I stepped into white snow,
powdered and clean
on the ground, as if it had fallen off moths' wings,
branches glistening and clear with white ice,
even my breath feeling white in my mouth,
and did not regret leaving the land of gardens at all.

Until this evening,
reading a plant magazine, and seeing an ad
saying,
"Sleep on a flower bed"
with a photo of a bed covered with a white spread and surrounded

53

by white flowers,
and read on to the words
which made me catch my white breath,
"imagine going to sleep with the smell of gardenias."

*   *   *

For I did
often
in these past four months on Molokai
come home with huge moth-winged white gardenias
from your giant bush,
and always
would put one (oh, the luxury, or even two . . .)
in a glass by my bed
and smell them, as I lay there reading,
smell the fragrance each time I'd wake up during those heavy
nights.

But in this icy world
where fragrance is frozen too,
I imagine often that there are ice gardenias
on my balcony
and I can pluck one as Jackie's Twelve Dancing Princesses did,
like a bunch of diamonds or rubies from some winter-enchanted
        branch
and place it in crystal by my downy, velvety bed,
the fragrance so etherealized
that I would only know it is there
matching my own white breath
by a whisper.
Cold, invisible, perfect.
A winter flower.
Not death, but its opposite.
White.
White.

CAP OF DARKNESS

For Robinson Jeffers

He walks on the desert at night,
which is a cool place,
moisture condensing on the succulent green bodies
of suaguero and cholla.
Alone, he should be aware of the city street
just a mile away,
and the city beyond that street,
the violence of hot bodies,
but he is

dreaming of a place where paradoxical landscapes
come together.

I repudiate the bad voices of my times,
and I repudiate the weak voices whose lyrics are better than their
          judgments.
So, I walk
in the desert
wearing the cap of darkness which I need only in the
city, but
like a reverse hero
                    (perhaps, that is what a woman is?
                    a reverse hero?)
I walk naked and unarmed in the city,
putting on the protective cap of darkness only when I
am alone,
in the desert.

How else would I have any honor?
For I am fighting the unknown, the invisible, the

ignorance of vision.
I do not need the beautiful silvery invisible helmet
to combat the Bostonian anaemic fashion-
mongers who worship fortune on the stockmarket or
the names of old families.
I do not need it to fight fake Zen-masters or
arrogant Quakers
or even the key holders to old university gates.

No, my battle is with
the ghosts themselves who have positioned
the false singers in their ancestral houses and given them
position, money and power.

The ghost of greed
is a Rational Man, with a good body, a sharp brain,
and a very comfortable life.
He offers me a place in one of these old brownstones
if I will accept his other converts.

But I will never convert to ghost life,
even though my battle
out here on the desert
is with ghosts and half-formed beings.
Wearing the cap of invisibility
which covers my silvery moonlike hair
without anything but a book for a weapon
and an orange for temptation

                    (birds, birds, with gold wings).

He walks in the desert at night,
where silence is an ally.
The city has muggers, rapists, and murderers
who edit periodicals, run contests
and serve themselves banquets.
Peace, peace,

I counsel,
no battles are worth the self-destruction,
but on the desert, there is a kind father who must be repudiated,
a sad mother who must be buried,
a jealous sister who will steal the silvery helmet,
and an inadequate lover
who will, unknowingly, give power
from his false use of moonlight
and his ignorance of the sun;

alone, alone,
not peace, but the battle with fashion
conducted in a place where glittering cities rise and
fall, with the breath of a sleeping person.

Who is that person?
The sleeping one
whose breath patterns so much?

The man who walks on the desert at night,
so close to the city,
not knowing the city itself,
but himself becoming the blazing lights,
the dark buildings with scattered illuminated windows,
and I, standing there,
invisible,
even though the helmet of night now belongs to a thief,
knowing the truth,
seeing the city and the desert as one
finally accepting the sand as my carpet,
the light as my hair,
the snakes as companions,
living in a city of cactus
which holds all the moisture needed
                              for existence.

LADY'S SLIPPER

paph-eye-o-pad-ill-um
small yellow shoe

open mouth/ sweet lips/ it is everything/ hand and foot.

As we lay in bed
two blocks from the rustling night ocean
under the disputed quilt
listening to two men screaming
in a lovers' quarrel

that overheard life seemed so thin with pain
and I felt safe in our normal love.

But you are gone now,
and I confess in my new life I love flowers
more than jewels or gold or men.

Just the color of this Concolor opening next to my bed.
This small soft flower
which will last
only a few weeks
but will bloom again every year, with care,
in my own house.

Dry earth,
its crust granular,
cracker crumbs on the sheets,
bare patches of it where grass will not grow,
yet a world
where dry sticks flower,
the golden branch
to be held in any gardener's hand;

the secrets old
                    poor
houses
yield, whispers in the dark,
the closet where we laylowformeddlers,
hidden,
the back porch with the scorched wall
where a trash fire ignited while I slept,
the living room shut off from children's sleeping alcove with a
        faded cotton curtain
where my mother met a man
who I thought was Santa Claus one Christmas Eve,
and outside, the spider-covered corner
of the house
where a calla lily
white as dead hands
bloomed perfectly;
its duck–bill yellow stamen as thick
as my 6-year-old finger
was covered with white cornmeal-like dust.
It was a flower for old women,
but the only secret I myself had
in that old shack of secrets;
my mother

who was no Leda
with her prematurely white hair
made her life
a mystery.
One which contained blood,
ashes, and the rose
of sex.
My childhood secret
was the calla lily,
an elderly, funereal flower
which smelled like the clean faded
under-garments in my
grandmother's
        aunts',
           and old mother's
               dresser drawers.

NELL'S BIRTHDAY

After the feast of Grandma's Tofu,
                    Shrimps in Barbeque Sauce,
                    Eggplant in Ginger Sauce,
                    Smoked Pork and Dumplings,
                    Beef with Broccoli,
and after the very European Strawberry Shortcake which L.W.
       made
and on which she placed
13 candles,
all of which you blew out in one breath,
and after Mark had given you the copy of Rhona Barrett's *How to*
       Achieve Wealth
and Sexual Ecstasy, personally inscribed,
and Marilyn had given you some coupons for free ice cream at
       Baskin-Robbins,
and after the more mundane things, and the bottles of wine, and
       Jim's bottle of
scotch,
       and you had begun to smoke up the carton of Benson &
       Hedges Phyllis
brought you, and after Anita and Rob had left to go and listen to
the radio broadcast of John Ashbery's poetry reading,
and you had declared friendship for all,
and 10-year-old Sarah, sweet little girl who cannot read, had seen
       Marilyn's
tortoise-shell comb in the shape of a shark and declared her passion
       for it,
then
       we left the Maple Gardens
                    and went out into the night made
                    cool
only by trade winds;

to be driven home in Jim's large Oldsmobile.

The front seat was large enough for four. Jim was as silent
as his car's push-button windows,
and the car was as large as Americans like to imagine all sharks.
You climbed into the back seat with your daughter, Sarah;
we drove home through neon Honolulu,
Jim quietly chauffeuring,
I, the visitor, trying to maintain my differences,
and not be absorbed into the landscape,
and you huddled in the back seat with your daughter,
so empty and quiet.

I am sure it was not the pain of 42 years creating your silence.
Rather, I felt as I once felt before,
that Death was the driver, taking us down Morning Street, down
Evening Street, through the silence of a gutted city.
I felt we drove into the River Styx.

Relieved to be let off at the Kaimana Beach Hotel,
like a reversal of the myth, I *could not* look back,
knowing that black car
with you huddled in the back seat, holding your sad daughter,
had a destination different from my own.
One you chose to go to.
And one from which you would not return.

Once up in my room, I sat on the balcony, watching the dark ocean,
thinking of you, as in the myth;
could any of us go where you are?
bargain for at least part
of your life?
To allow you, even, to appear yearly,
along with the narcissus,
the crocus, beautiful flower from which saffron is made,
and Wordsworth's daffodil?

Would this relieve at all that night?
When you were in a large black car,
being driven in the music of silence,
                              no lyre,
                                    no voice even,
surrounded by a city
of
drowned sailors?

DIRECTIONS

The compass which I bought for my car
is a disappointment.
It is I
who must find true north
and by elaborate motions
and mechanical twistings
set the compass
so that it will record direction.
                              Another myth about
the autonomy of scientific instruments
sliding away.
The compass only recording the North when I fix the North.
And the inevitable.
My observation of
the sun's rising east and setting west required
to make the instrument operative.

What do I know about you?
whose name is always next to my teeth?
I call you a childish nickname
                         Key?
                              Key?

Where is my key?

Listening to a friend who cares for me
I know that she doesn't understand
the immense drama or any of the mystery.
She needs a secret lover
yet cannot accept the truly forbidden.

I want to slip a noose around the necks of those beautiful men
who make love
to other men

and mock woman's sacrificing body.
She is right: I cannot do that.
The other Diane who loved her Freddie, dancing off the edge of a
       roof
into champagne death,
how did she continue to embrace, even marry,
sodomists?
Their soft necks,
those beautiful boys,
how I would like to hurt them.

You are right, Judy,
no one wants to hear.
But I want to speak.
I want you to listen.

What difference does it make
how a driver finds the direction of true North?

MEMORY

Your face in the first row,
like an old shiny leather ball,
tight, compact, lined & greased.

The expensive hair cut,
the fashionable clothes on your thin tree body,
the deep voice —
           do you drink secretly?

Wondering what this rich matron
more appropriate to Connecticut or Scarsdale
can be doing at a mid-Western poetry reading
a somewhat provincial event.

Then, later, we talk
and it is as if we have always been friends.
We are as natural as two leaves
which fell off the same branch.

My own vanity which for years I disguised
in humble posture, plain clothes,
straight hair, not wearing makeup,
and in fact talking about contempt for the body
which can never represent
the complexity or beauty inside.
                        The fact
that until 40, I looked young and fresh, even
girlish.
I look every year that I am, now.
Have to finally acknowledge vanity
to discard it.
Terribly aware of looking fat, middle-aged, and dowdy,
I marvel when people come up to me after a program and say,

"You look wonderful," or
"You haven't changed a bit";

photos must lie.
Or most people don't see others.
For, I do not look the same,
and my health is poor,
and surely,
someone must notice that I
who always looked like a young girl
now look
like a middle-aged woman?

And you, who looked so old
while oiling your face to look young and tan,
you, have changed too. You
                              look
younger than I; or am I used to
you? Which camera snapped the right
picture?
What do we look like?
Why are we cursed with these bodies?
Or is it memory
we should blame?

ADVENTURES ON A BALCONY OVERLOOKING
THE MORNING OCEAN

Jim Wright,
Li Po of Manhattan,
I think of you when this almost two-inch bee
comes whirling through the air
as beautiful to me
as the water ouzel I saw splashing and playing
in Barbara Drake's Oregon stream
this summer
while everyone else was hiking and I sat on the bank
looking for stones and thinking of your poetry
which swirls around me now
unusual and perfect as this bee this morning near the ocean.

The ocean peaceful before a coral reef,
and breaking in white slashes beyond and this morning
presenting still life as subject for art,
the large bee which I love for its bumble and fuzz
its uniqueness on my porch
with the palms creaking like dry leather below,
the sound of the ocean which you
and some others
have translated,
given, yes, the pear blossoms floating on water
a cup of tea I lift to my lips
the ones which drink poetry
in each cup, the moon,
to embrace,
I thank you, Jim Wright,
I thank the bumble bee.

MEASURING

*(On hearing that the gorilla in the Honolulu Zoo
has a television set, and that he beat up his mate so
badly that the officials, to solve the problem of not
being able to put a gorilla in traction, bought her a
waterbed on which they both lie, now, while
watching television)*

I can begin the morning with geometry

the way the waves break each morning
at the same location.
Sitting on my balcony
with compass and protractor
from my high school geometry class
I could measure the distance
and the foam faithfully would break
not a hair farther out.

Even when
the sea is rough,
each line of foam
slanting perfectly out towards the horizon.

A block away
in a city zoo
the mountain gorilla,
                    someone has told me,
has been given a television set.
It is turned on all the time,
and I see it with white noise and static
frequently showing only abstract patterns from the minds of physi-
        cists.

"Does the gorilla watch any shows?" I asked.

No, my friends say, he often sits with his back to it, sulking,
the way gorillas sulk, you know.

Do they? I think to myself.
No wonder.
In their bare arenas of concrete.
These animals are at home
in bamboo forests. They shyly live long lives,
hidden by leaves.

I think then of inviting gorillas in from all the world zoos
to my apartment, with its rattan bamboo furniture,
and its rain forest carpeting,
with its jungle of ferns and begonias,
orchid and anthurium.
An apartment in which I refuse to keep a TV.

One gorilla could sit in the corner of the bright yellow and cane divan.
He could sit staring at the asparagus fern
(which has reached the floor several times and each time been trimmed)
while I type in the next room,
stopping occasionally to go to the kitchen for a cup of tea.
I would see him sitting there for hours,
staring,
while a Mozart symphony plays on the stereo.
I, writing letters to my friends,
each in his own cage
or bamboo forest
or zoo.

My own body. Uncooperative.
Rough.
An Asian girl with a diamond in one nostril.

And now I see two white rubber-capped heads, bobbing in this
today-predictable place.

Are they swimmers?
Or could they be some new way of measuring
the certainty of the sea?

TROPHIES

For a man who learned to swim
when he was sixty

To you,
the ocean was like an old mother, saying,
      "Leon, why can't you be more like Abe?
      He's such a good boy
      playing quietly at his little table.

      (Leon is such a rascal.
      He's never still.)"

And you walked into the blue water,
the sand as white as your mother's ankle.
The palm trees leaning,
like old people talking to each other.

Deeper, deeper,
you walk till it's above your waist.

      "Leon," calls your mother
whose voice is now the breakers
crashing out beyond you in the ocean,
beyond this sheltered bay.

      "Leon, be careful.
      I know you'll do something clever
      and get yourself into trouble."

There is no way you can swim.
For sixty years the water speaks
like a mother whom you beautifully obey.

72

You too, a palm tree, bending to listen carefully
for each word.

Silence
was your answer until
one day
you walked into water,
and the immense white beach was not her braceleted hand
caressing your feet, making love to your own white body.

I do not really know your story.
But I do know
that at some point the angry voice
her teeth
her stunning white ankle that you feared
became beautiful.

As trophies,
you fought for them, possessed them.

It is too simple to say
a woman taught you to swim.

Let us say, instead, that your enemy did.
As the Indians tell us,
it is our enemies/
fighting them/
articulating and defining what we despise or eschew,

our enemies
who make us heroes.

WHAT I LEARNED ABOUT THE WORLD FROM BARRY LOPEZ

For William Stafford

When I walked in the shape of an elk
I did not recognize myself and, in fact, I still wonder/

I saw you walking with cumulus clouds over your head and
        shoulders
like the ones I see over the waters of Puget Sound and hovering
around Mt. Baker.

Without changing reality
I want to specify how much your clouded head attracted me,
my fascination with the legs walking defined
and carrying something which was hidden and I could not define.

I thought, of course, a man was inside the cloud bank. It was a
        man's
legs
I saw.
And at times, knowing of my own confused identity,
I thought it might be a man with the head of a dog,
or perhaps,
an elk,
maybe a buffalo. I even thought of Max Ernst:
a man with the head of a lion. Or some vision of Magritte's:
a man with the head of an apple.

Today, when you walked in
with that snowy bank of clouds surrounding the place where your
head should be,
I wondered if maybe you were Ubu.
A few years ago I thought you might be a coyote or even

the spirit of Marcel Duchamp, a student or disciple of his.

This week I moved into a house with you. You lived
in the room next door. I saw your legs walking down stairs and I
saw you going into the bathroom, your head always in clouds—
Mt. Ranier, Mt. Olympus, Mt. Angeles.

Is this a mistake?
I think your head *is* the clouds.
I think you are someone with a man's legs and torso
but hovering above that,
no neck, no head,
simply a rich foamy bank of clouds.
Why do I hate them?
They are beautiful.
Want to attack them?
Dissolve them or make them part, just once, to reveal a head?
Even at worst, like Washington Irving's catskill ghost,
a man without a head.

Last night the storyteller told us
about ghost bison, larger than elephants and white,
living in the Cascade Mountains. Just as I was falling asleep
I heard him say that a great man
loves his enemy,
for the enemy allows him to see
what it is he must battle,
allows him,
forces him,
to fight for the good he believes in,
and thus to his enemy he owes his heroism.

As I fell asleep in the room next door to yours,
falling asleep with the words of the storyteller clarifying
my night,
I saw you
walking up the stairs into your room, still a pair of legs, a shirt,

and a tower of white clouds above.
I said to myself, "Forget everything else.
The man with clouds for a head is your enemy. Honor him.
Battle him. Love him.
He will make you a hero."

A CALIFORNIAN FIGHTS AGAINST THE OLD
NEW ENGLAND TRADITIONS

To Stanley Kunitz

The elderly famous man goes shopping with me at the Safeway
and while I am filling my cart with the most interesting cheeses
I can find
(alas, not many)
and searching for good mustard and other exotics,
I see him
in his sailor's cap and small safari jacketed shoulders
bending over the margarines, comparing
prices, looking for sales;
we move together to the coffee aisle and while I spot the
          Columbian
—in a can—lament that our vacation house does not have a
coffee grinder,
feel complacent that I have brought my own teapot and can of
Fortnum & Mason Ceylon Tea,
I notice that he is peering at all the prices,
and finally choosing the can of coffee whose price is the most
          spare:
Edwards Brothers.

We move over to soups,
and I finally get tired of watching.
Rebelliously, youthfully (tho I am forty), I say,
"No wonder I will never get rich. I can't bear all this comparing."

During the week, I discover that he cooks well,
though I hate losing supremacy in the kitchen. Yet,
his thirty years of seniority makes me feel like withdrawing over
and over again.

When he reads manuscripts,
I think of his small figure bent over the Safeway prices,
comparing, looking for the most economical.
I ask myself whether my values represent only the wastrel,
his, the efficient?

No answer, but an understanding of what constitutes extravagance.
If I spend too much, then
by the same token, I think he spends too little.

Now, I have to condemn myself, though,
for looking at a frail old-man's life
and letting my own gimlet eyes
give him so little.

"Where is your extravagance now, Westerner?" I ask myself.
"Who is being stingy, giving up excellence in favor of easy
          bargains?"

Ashamed of my own lack of generosity
still I must hold the accusation, meanly.
A young Californian rebelling against New England,
knowing my origins are from hot countries.
lands unlike Massachusetts or New York,   lands
where the huge mountains
are deeply packed with precious minerals,
even gold.
Where everything is big,
with the space of the desert,
big, like I want to be.

CIVILIZATION

I admire all the brave and robust people who live on shoestrings,
somehow crafting interesting meals out of dollar bills,
drinking a passable wine for a quarter,
building houses out of old telephone poles and getting featured in
     Better Living.
They go to Europe and meet the most interesting people and
somehow earn a refund,
go to the opera in thrift store drapes and get photographed for
the society page.
Somehow, they work twenty hours a day, never sleep, have the
     most
beautiful children,
get lots of sex, write novels in their spare time, tune their own
cars,
and like Mildred Pierce bake 100 pies every day, even the day
their ten-year-old
dies of pneumonia in the hospital.

I have always been poor, and never managed well.
I took taxis when I was tired and thus had no money for food
halfway through
the week. The mediocre wines on my table cost as much as
emerald necklaces,
and I always look like I live on welfare.

I suppose this will sound like self-pity,
but I think it is only facing facts and not liking that reality.
The language of pain is difficult to transmit;
it is the glorious nature of civilization to reject suffering.

PACHELBEL'S CANON

I was like a pearl in a Japanese fisherman's pocket.
I felt a small luster.
Nacre was in my eyes.

In the Los Angeles bookstore
with tables of books like fields of vegetables
we must walk through towards the back room,
you and Martha and Greg and me.
Reading is difficult
in front of the few listeners.
Your hands did blossom into blood and roses
a string of irregular pearls, long enough for a wreath
the oddly shaped bits of nacre
like squash seed with bad genes
twisting their way out of preposterous crooked vegetables.

The music should have meant nothing.
Background.
But I sleep in Denver and wake up with roses wetting my lips.

You are alone and not near me.
The empty house of Gothic parody attracts me
I am not a pearl or a bloody rose
I am a woman who loved a man who could not love her.

Against everyone's dream advice,
I go into the Gluckish house, wishing I would will Mary Stewart
and other Lady Romancers not to enter my dreams.
I am trying to keep some distance
for I know I should not go into the house.

I go right to the bathroom.
I am with a kind friend who wants to spare me.

He cannot keep me from looking in the door.

Something I shall never forget.
My own image which haunts me more than the real you.
Naked in the bathtub, your tall body
which I loved so much, with its strange hairlessness and boyish
breasts (you never really looked manly without clothes)
and now you are lying grotesquely in the empty tub
with your head wired up to the ceiling,
the throat cut,
you covered with blood.
I did not look at your penis, for some reason,
but at your feet with those strange long delicate beautiful toes.
I wondered if the blood was really out of your typewriter
or some huge falling of roses.

The scene was awful and yet acceptable.
The blood of your shame seemed inevitable.
And I woke up in Denver away from the unbloody you
to that piece of music.

Walking in the Los Angeles bookstore where you and
Martha will read to an audience of five
we all ask the name of that piece of music
(which two years ago was debased for use as background in a
TV commercial)
Pachelbel's Canon.

I do not know why I chose the irregular pearls.
Perhaps because George Washington might have given them to
his mother
after his own teeth were lost.

The porcelain bathtub, the gleaming ideal plumbing,

I cannot know —
if sometimes we wash too much of the blood and shit away
down the sewers.

Unfinished.
The story is unfinished.

WASHING & IRONING

They were hanging clothes out
on the line
    I said to myself,
"I never want to live this way again."

Waking up in California at 7 a.m. in December
when it is dark.
The light in the next room, like a spoiled bottle of milk
in an empty refrigerator, tells me
my mother is ironing in the kitchen.
She irons white lacy blouses,
long-sleeved blue business shirts,
linen pillow cases.
The room is filled with cotton and linen,
smelling new and fresh; her iron has smoothed
everything till it is like paper.
There are stacks and hangers.
She has been ironing since 4:30 a.m. and she
gets dressed to go to work at the water company
where she is a bookkeeper. The ironing
she will deliver to the woman who employs her
for $10 a week to iron.

And I hate this, locked into my helpless
child-life, knowing my mother works all
day
as a bookkeeper, then irons at night
simply to pay our rent. And I am angry,
and say I will never learn to keep
accurate
records,
never type,
and never iron clothes
when I am adult.
The off-white image

83

of spoiling milk.

* * *

Humiliation.
The pain of helplessly watching someone else suffer.
An anger at the old servitudes.

* * *

Waking up to see morning glories in the window
and to see the early morning sunshine coming
in the door, hearing
the morning doves making their throaty noises
and my mother standing in our small living room
ironing the sundresses covered
with carnations my sister and I will wear
this summer Southern California morning.
I smell the hot wet cotton
and feel the luxury of being in bed with a
whole fresh summer day stretching ahead of me
like a newly baked loaf of bread.

* * *

Wondering about Helen
who comes to our two-room shack in the orange grove, with the
sagging screened porch.
She and my mother slept on the couch
which was made into a bed at night.
Innocent children.
Innocent women.
My anger at the poor life,
at spoiled milk,
at this woman who crowded our house.

* * *

We have a washing machine with an electric wringer.
How I hate those rollers flattening out
the clothes into scraps each wash day.

Most of all, I hate hanging the clothes on the line.
And I hate the feel of the stiff clothes when
they are dry, and I hate taking off the clothespins which *thunk* into
        the
clothespin bag, the smell of pasture
in the board-stiff cloth.
How I love electric dryers which have
liberated me from the clothesline.
Poor housemaid,
hanging out the clothes,
poor woman,
along comes a blackbird and snips off
her nose.

*   *   *

And I want to tell everyone in these primitive
Sandwich Islands
how much I detest seeing clothes
hanging on a line
how unsuitable to the 20th century
it seems
that women should hang out clothes
over the wet red clay mud
and bring them in, stiff and reddish.
The deliberate refusal to use electricity
when it is there
to make life cleaner, more convenient.
Deliberately choosing the drab afternoons
hanging wet clothes on a line, and the
unsatisfactory feel and smell of the clothes
hanging out in muddy, windy, smokey
yards.
The fact that a seven-year-old boy
who had to hang out the washing on the line
was taunted by an eight-year-old boy
for doing woman's work, and the
seven-year-old boy went into the house

85

and got his father's automatic
pistol and shot the taunting eight-year-old
to death
      seemed
hideously
in keeping
with my feelings about that awful anachronism:
the deliberate refusal to own an electric dryer
(or to use it, if one owned one),
and the clinging to that hideous practice,
hanging the washing out
on a clothesline.
Hanging
Sour milk.
Hanging.

*   *   *

Oh, how glad I am to sit with my book or pen and paper
at the laundromat,
while the warm air gushes around the fabrics,
rotating them smooth, airing them,
drying them warm and supple.
How I embrace the 20th century and its technology,
freeing me from centuries of drudgery,
relieving a little the memory
of my mother's early morning ironing
which she did as uselessly
as they still hang out the washing
on Molokai/ an act of will,
plus the acknowledgment of ingenious brains;

and we *do* have a choice now.
We can leave savage customs behind.

SEARCHING FOR THE CANTO FERMO

For Norman Hindley

> *Moon, moon,*
> *when you leave me alone,*
> *all the darkness*
> *is an utter blackness.*
>
> — *Robert Creeley,*
> *"A Form of Women"*

Preface: Thoth, an ibis standing on one leg, or a dog-headed baboon, was given the moon, a gift created especially for him by Ra, when Thoth searched in the desert and returned to Ra his Eye, who had run away, in the form of the beautiful woman, Tefnut. His own eye, then, Thoth's the moon, that litchi nut. And Nut (noot)—that woman stretched out, her elongated body arched over the earth so that only her toes and fingertips touched her husband, Geb, the earth—Nut, Night, tall woman was be-friended by Thoth, who felt sorry that Ra, jealous, decreed that Nut would not be able to bear children during any month of the year. The wily old dog-headed baboon, Thoth, he played dice with the moon, and won from him a seventy-second part of his light. Five days, on that 360-day lunar calendar, and on each of these days, respite from the rest of the year, Nut could give birth. So, she and Geb had their children after all: Isis, Osiris, Horus, Set, and Napthys. Gifts of the moon.

Norman,
the moon, like Mary-Beth's pleasing savories,
(litchi nuts stuffed with cream cheese
that has been studded with candied ginger),

unites us in our search
for communication,
that perfect word,
the measurer of time,
in Egypt, (or California or Hawaii) holding a palm branch,
sometimes a silver bow
and arrows made of children's bones. Do men and women
see the same moon in the sky?

Sometimes I wonder if there is not a form of woman
which is closer to man than to that tall long-toed and -fingered
woman,
Night,
Nut,
arching over the earth like an eel,
giving birth to five hell-raising children.
Not Sapphic woman, loving other women,
but somehow that image of the cool hidden form in the rain forest
of your rescue, Norman;
the huntress with silver bow and arrow,
the goddess of chastity or virginity, which did not mean
abstinence from sex, but rather, an unmarried woman.

The moon in that Egyptian world was a man,
a gambler,
though in so many other places
moon is woman,
but never woman of the hearth,
never woman of food and nourishing meals.
Just as the great chefs of Europe are men,
the moon was a gambling man on the Nile.

I have never been able to make myself into that wife and mother,
that woman of the hearth,
though I love to cook
and I do not make love to other women.
I have felt myself often

as that presence hidden behind the palm ferns.
I have felt myself the gambler on the Nile who felt sorry for Nut,
and let Thoth win for her a seventy-second part of my light
in order to give her babies.
I understand that giving of fertility and of sharing.
But when I have felt myself hunting, I have been terrified
at what you so calmly accepted,
shooting the mother turkey in her nest,
knowing as a woman, that turkey could be me;
oh, but what I have not felt
is some perfect combination of the word, the belly, and the hand,
and in giving birth, felt only the blood,
the pain,
the meaningless result.
When my hand reaches out to take one of those juicy litchi nuts
with ginger and cream cheese, I suddenly become
the eye, the moon, see myself in a different form,
the one you sensed in the forest,
and feel the big teeth enclosing my own form.
Norman,
the moon unites us.
I, not quite woman,
you, not quite man, with that voice singing out of you like babies
popping out ofyour mouth, their fat little hands holding the bow
and arrow for you,
so that you too can hide behind the ferns in the cool rain forest;

a word: that
is the huntress.
The word which is the venison you shot,
marinated in soy sauce, tequila and ginger,
the word which is fresh mangoes,
the word—white sashimi you pulled out of the ocean that
         morning,
the word in the hand-warmed glass of California cabernet.

If the moon is not spoken,

then there is no speech. Neither man nor woman invented it;
speech is what is left,
like the footprint,
after the body is gone,
what is made out of the food chewed by the big teeth,
touched by the soft lips,
the Phillipine chilies arousing the throat,
all nourishment in the belly,
becomes words,
the lost five days of light
which the moon generously lost
to let Nut have her rebellious children.
Yes, Creeley, there is a form of women which will never leave
        you alone
as long as you make a word.
That word comes out of you
as you see light on the silver bow,
the glint of that moving silver arrow,
the swift death which becomes meat,

the celebration of eating, drinking, reading:
the beautiful woman with a
silver foot.

A CHRISTMAS POEM WRITTEN FOR BLACK SPARROW PRESS:
ABALONE

a sure footing,
the jeweled slipper
on the stair

The tight dry landscape
of California.
The tight dry landscape
of CHRIST
        mass,
            not for poetry.
No dew on these steps/ like pearls.
A pound of pearls.

Nor the savory resin
of pine boughs
          were they
tacked to doors
to invite the season?
The sap of the branches,
snapping into cold, into snow. No,
this is not that landscape.

Mother of Pearl,
the thick milk of shell,
iridescent, graceful lyric of bone/mineral   observa-
tions
the moments,
multiply.

The tight dry sounds
of winter

recur
even in this season
at this beach
which never knew
its winter
force.

                        California divers
go down with their knives
sever abalone
a rubber foot
in its jewel case.
                And when low tide comes,
I suppose,
(in months containing the letter "r")
the diver
does not even have to
dive.
        What makes us want to pontificate,
        make rules after the fact,
        or for that matter,
        before?

M. hears Amelia Earhart
                  "shhhhhhhhhhhhhhh," he says to me,
"she may be among us now . . ."
and I look
for some reason why
I feel so much anger towards the world.
What did it give?—
that I should resent
when it's taken away?
             I think of an old
acquaintance
a woman who had a bank account
when we were both novice jr high school teachers
who now has no

                    bank account,
                              and I,
losing the one property I ever tried to buy; stripped,
no more debts,
no credits either.

Remembering,
tonight remembering,
a dancer named Duncan
(that was his first name)
not because of what he did as a dancer,
but that he made me one, once. For a moment
I walked
barefoot
through Dwinelle Plaza
a student's recreation yard, a place for
scholars to gather, the Roman forum.

He gave me a wicker birdcage to carry.
Surely, it was a dance,
for everyone who saw/
understood something about body.
I became the girl who walked through Dwinelle Plaza, barefoot
on a cool afternoon,
carrying an empty birdcage, as if it were a lantern, held high
in front of me.

Some of us should have become makers
of movies,
some, corporate presidents.
But all of us became poets.
And what do you thank of that, Mr. Possum?

*   *   *

Abalone.
We had abalone for a snack last night.

A mistake,
one toiled over. And a star
fell
burning
out of my mouth. Oh, friends,
I am dying,
just like you,
piece by piece.
No peace, tho.
Always, we are fighting.

*   *   *

for Creeley

The tight dry sounds
of winter
recur.
     My tan heels
disappearing around the mussel–studded rocks.

In middle–age
which we all eventually stumble to,
the edges of our decadent lives curl,
old, tattered, brittle,
like newspaper accounts of
youthful triumphs.   Winter
comes
like a flute solo
emerging from medieval music
                          What is the moon?
It used to drip from my fingers.
Don't ask me how earth binds,
for I know frozen ground
or ground filled with clay. I know winter
which came
like crystals in my joints
rheumatism at age 10.

Robert,
(like George, you are one of American's most common names)
Robert Creeley,
winter baron,
reminder of all other Roberts, robbers.
                                        Can di-
gression, as you say,
be a structure in itself? The only real
narrative?
Everything,
a spiraling out
within the space
                    (of our minds?).

*   *   *

The tight dry sounds of winter
recur.
Thank God for Yule, the time of eating and drinking,
largesse and oblivion.
                        The tight dry sounds
of ocean,
winter,
life,
push at the arms of the divers (diverse,
diver's press)   the pressure
to breathe

it covers us all.

SHE TAKES THE SCISSORS

She takes the scissors to the grapevine and snips.

I don't want them to leave each other.
He will be alone without her.
She had violence in her voice.
He had precision.

What a perfect combination.

Why are they leaving each other?

The summer trellis fills with the smell of Concords,
purple, slightly dusted,
the cool juice.
The silver scissors cuts bunch after bunch
to go into the leaf-lined basket.

Sipping a chilly chablis
the glass beading up,
I indulge in the reality of fiction,
those lives I cannot change or touch.
My friends are far more remote than Isabella Archer
whose life, of course,
I cannot change.

24 June 1972

Dear J————,

I don't have any idea if this mail I send ever gets out of Mexico, but I suppose it is another of my gestures of faith that I write and send it, in spite of that gamble.

I must tell you about my big scare last night. I was sure that my window (only on the second floor here) was being broken into, and that I was going to be 1)raped, 2)robbed, 3)murdered, and/or 4)frightened to death. I suppose that my main reason for thinking so is the way Mexican men stare at women. It gives me the creeps, as if we were religious idols that they want a blood sacrifice from, or as if they've been hypnotized to stare at us, or somehow as if they have never seen or desired women before. Anyway, it's very unsettling. With Clayton and Caryl I never need to go anywhere by myself. I feel safe and anticipate a cloistered time when I go without them to Puerta Vallerta, where I will go from the dining room to the swimming pool to my room back to the dining room and to bed. I hope I'll be a little bolder than that, and go at least to one other restaurant and perhaps the beach. But I'm not sure right now how I'll react alone.

Anyway, last night about 2 a.m., I woke with the proverbial start, hearing someone/something at my window, which I knew was closed and behind venetian blinds as well as drapes. But I heard the scraping, as if someone was trying to open the catch. I jumped out of bed, turned on all the lights, took my big wooden key in hand, made sure my papers and money were safe and stood there waiting for the worst, wondering if I should run next door and get Clayton and Caryl, or what I should do. I decided to open the

97

door to the corridor and slam it shut, so that whoever was out there would not only see all my lights come on, but would also know that I was able to walk out into the hall. Well, the noises stopped, I got back into bed, decided to read for awhile and finally fell asleep with all the lights blazing and my glasses on.

Let me explain, that I am very frightened of the dark and of being alone. It has been one of my great disciplines of the last few years to make myself turn off all the lights in an apartment or house when I am alone, but I still humor myself if I'm very nervous, by leaving one light, usually in the bathroom, on, to reassure me. I feel safer in hotels than elsewhere, except in the houses of real people (families), but often still have to leave some light on. I've been very good for the past week and a half and have been able to sleep without leaving any lights on. But my daytime fierceness totally deserts me when I am alone at night. Many things frighten me, and I have spent a large portion of my life trying to conquer my fears, many of them successfully, but in times of stress they all come back.

At 4 a.m., I awoke again, sharply, hearing the same sounds at the window. Once again I got up and went through my previous ritual, lay down to read some more and when the sounds had ceased for about 10 minutes, I decided to lift the drapes to see if there was anyone or anything outside the window to explain the noise. I stood away from the window and lifted the drape, and saw the venetian blind which had its slats open, move. I saw there was no figure of person or animal or anything big enough to be dangerous out there, so I gently lifted the tip of the venetian blind. Out into the window recess, but still behind the drape, flew an enormous dusky moth, about 5 inches wide, half of his wing torn from beating against the blind where he had been caught. Not knowing what to do, I left him behind the drapes but liberated from the blinds. He is still alive, tho near death I am sure, still occasionally moving in the corner of my window. He is beautiful, and I think there is a certain madness in my marauder turning out to be a butterfly—for, if I had to choose two symbols for myself, one would be the moon and the other would be a butterfly.

When I was a child, I used to stand for hours, abnormally still for a child of five, in front of a hedge of lantana and catch butterflies in my bare fingers, something no child should have been able to do. In retrospect, I can only think that I must have been almost catatonic as a child, that I could stand or sit for hours, without talking or moving, thinking, some strange poetry making life bearable to me.

I constantly think of you as someone with no fears who started out in life the opposite from me, having no mad hurdles of fright to jump, having life in some way cut out for you; and of how strange it is that we have turned out to be such similar people, for very few people in the world see that I have not always been confident and sure of myself, that I have not always been aggressive and able to work for what I want. The me which is in my poems is the double me. Always believing personally in my own beauty and strength, at the same time, never thinking anyone else could ever perceive it or that the world would honor it.

I cannot explain to you the spiritual journey which allowed me to come to where I am now, but can only say that if you care about me, you must always understand that under that strong Diane who is witty and funny and who wears bright colors and jokes about everything, who stomps through the world with leather boots and pants and whose tongue is sharp enough to cut diamonds, there is still the child who was afraid of fire, water, dark and loneliness, as there is always the child somewhere in all of us, and the man I will love is the man who will honor my adult strength while not provoking my childhood fears.

We are going to Chickenitza tomorrow, and then back to Mexico City for two days. Since I carry my own world with me wherever I go, it doesn't really make any difference to me where I am. Tho I prefer sun and water to other landscapes.

The Moth

It was brown and dusty,
with peacock eyes,
marbled black tracings,
wings
as wide as my hand across.
Trapped behind blinds,
      as they say the poet is the blind man,
      emphasizing the fact
      that what he sees
      is in the mind,
      not part of the world.
And the moth was trapped
and it had broken
enough of its wing
for me to understand death
in my room;
and I thought of you,
who are so much in my mind,
who have never been trapped,
never had to beat your wings against a blinding force,
never were the scraping at a woman's window
which made her fear
and you die.

The beauty of this simple white room
with its dark wood beams,
tile floors,
in a place where a butterfly the size of my hand
could fly in from the corridors
during the day
only to beat itself to death at night,

this beauty,
is only one part of a world
that has many parts
                    I long
for those parts I
do not have,
as we all love
what is part of the world we cannot be.

You don't/couldn't understand
what it is
that I love about you.
And if I told you,
you still would not understand.
I am trapped
by my own words, always,
the words which explain
and in explaining
lose love.

I told a man once
that his freedom would also be his death,
but he thought I was cursing him,
not saying the truth.
The truth has always trapped me.
It is brown and dusty.
With peacock eyes.
Marbled black tracings.
Its wings
as wide as my hand.

You are in my mind now,
but I do not think of that as a trap;
in the corner of my window,

the butterfly still moves,
though so much of his wing
has been torn away
now.

yrs,

Diane

I DREAM OF MY FAILURES WITH ED DORN AS JUDGE

The man with the guitar
disappeared
and in his place, the chef's hat.
But he carved open his own belly, seppuku,
and was finally of no use in the kitchen.

Then I walked to the mid-West
where I was always tired; for I had to dream of oceans
as there were none there,
and in reproducing the waves
and the power of tons of water circling the earth
I found myself weak
and ironically floating/tossed about
though we were on dry plain.

There was a potter
and I said hello to him.
How busy one can be with clay.

An age of paper men in dark hats rustled in mydoorway, invisible.
I did not fear them, though they would have destroyed me.
Only the plants now
give me some solace. People frequently call them
the wrong names,
but the only naming which counts
is that which
is done in silence.

Where is the West?

Wherever lantana grows.

103

How still can a child be? I know
now that children move and talk and
in fact are like fire and water
far more than adults.
But my own childhood was spent
as a ghost, whose words
came out thin, misty and almost silently.
I sat quietly,
so quietly that adults often forgot
I was there, and cut paper dolls
or read my book
but always listened,
and waited,
listened
with murdering stillness.

A long hedge of lavender flowerets,
the lantana with its dusty, slightly bitter
smell, the little dark berries forming
after the flowers, like the beady eyes of birds,
and the flowers themselves
like tiny cushions of bouquet.
How the Monarchs, Swallowtails and Cabbage Moths
loved this hedge, and the smaller greying moths with brown eyes
in their peasant wings; they would sit with blades moving
back and forth for balance, fanning,
almost underwater motions, their black scrolled etchings
calligraphing the whole yardfront hedge,
and I, age five, hypnotized by the orange and yellow
stained glass, fragile with powder,
would stand quietly
quietly, until the insects forgot
I was there; I stood still
looking, listening for whatever there was to hear,
the humming of the hedge, the hot afternoon buzzing

and cracking, my hands poised, thick little girl hands
but still,
still as stone,
more still than a child's hands could be
till the butterflies dazed with the quiet day and the heat
relaxed their fanning wings
then I slowly moved and would capture one, pinched between my
            small
thick fingers, and take it home, a prize
for a glass jar.

How did I do this? My hands that have shaken since adolescence
with nervous energy and mercurial power?
Yet, I still can sit for hours, without fidgeting.

Unnatural, though, that I in my little black high-topped shoes
with yellow braids pinned on top of my head that bees liked to sit
            on
should have started with this stillness.
It continues to be the most I have to offer/ this stillness.

Because of it
I was able to murder butterflies.
I didn't want them in glass jars, only wanted to
catch them. Didn't want to kill them/ only wanted to prove I
            could
catch them.
Pity me
in my little black shoes,
not knowing what to do
for love,
or beauty,
and that my murdering stillness was
all
I had to offer.

I want you to
Love me,
I sd.
But,
    I do,
He sd.

You cdn't or
You wdn't have done
Those things.

       The curtain
       The swallow wings in my throat
       The canyon hot under my foot
       A dry day
       Yr breath   the wind
                     of Santa Ana.

How do we ever know
What love means?
Do we even want it? What we need
Is some trust,
Some common ground,
The same touch,
Every night.

Sometimes the silence
is so much more than we deserve
like a pocket of time,
a crystal room we walk into
and suddenly find
as in the fairy tale.
We don't any longer see a door.
The room of mirrors where every wall
looks like an entrance or exit
but neither is actually there . . .

Sometimes the silence
is a presence in the room,
and all language proceeds from that.
The space you occupy —
I reverse the positive and negative;
I restrain my hand from obliterating you,
and accept the presence.
It is not silence but it bears some relation to it.
I begin, momentarily, to understand death,
though never violence, never shattering.

Sometimes the silence is like a cat who sits on vain laps,
knowing the exhibitionist
is the best lover. Is loss of vanity
death? Or at least its foreshadowing?

Oh, Creeley, does anybody know
how remarkable your poems are?
The most original prosodist of the 20th century,
and I point out that you are an ex-latin master,
the use of the Latin love lyric as model for strong Anglo-Saxon
        words.

And each day
I would have trouble resisting ferns, begonias, palms, an azalea, a
        rose, an
orchid, a lily, a calceolaria. Spring
of course,
would be the starting point.

Are we utterly condemned to be what we despise?
Am I Corman,
that petty man?

This empty room reminds me of a great man,
his early publisher,
and the fickle grasping nature of everyone except perhaps
the true poet.

(The girls here don't read William Stafford
and without his dilettante audience
I would even more be tempted to call him the Duchamp of the
        poetry world.
But even he
does not know how sly his own theories are. Oh, Jack
Spicer,
why were you so frightened.

Lose love,
and you lose fear?

Never let yourself be judged.
I've always had that discretion.
Each year I grow more silent
and find most words too crude for that art of precision.
When you finally have a tuned ear
then silence is the greatest music.
Silence, that symphony you deserve.

TO BE HAUNTED

The hiss of tires on the wet street
steams in through my window.
Something lies in my pocket
which changes the whole day.

Where are you;
it isn't even your letter which lies crumpled
there

a tiger with a marigold in his mouth
is walking along the sidewalk.
My past,
so far down the boulevard
we cannot see it.

It is the rain
and I think of Paris,
New Year's Eve,
getting off the train at the Gare du Nord,
sitting at a table in a loud cafe
with our bottle of champagne
and watching the oyster man shuck plates
and plates of *fruits de mer*
his big red hands wielding the knife
with the quick movements of a cat jumping from a window.

Why do I savor
what I have lost?
He's gone.
He's gone.
I am old/no
not old; simply not the same.

What do you do
when you read the name of a man
who used to live next door to you
and who was much admired by a man you once loved?
And that name is printed in a black square
where his death is announced
along with the deaths of two other people you once knew
and not at all fondly?
And you read those three names
and the announcement of their deaths
while you are lying in bed
having just spent an hour feeling angry
over your lack of worldly success
while you are sweating with a cold and fever?

What do you do
when you find that nothing in your life
has meant the same thing it meant to you
to anyone else?
What do you do
when you are almost
as afraid of life as
you are of death?
Where do you get energy from?
How do you keep going when you are weary?
When are weariness and laziness the same thing?
Why do memories punish you more than anything else?
Why does music move you to tears?
Why do you want to be Beethoven?
Why do you have no patience?

"They're a grateful plant,"
said a woman whom I despised.

Why did I despise her?
Because she let herself be cheated
and bragged about
how
the world took
advantage of her.

My petunias on the balcony
are flourishing
in this Michigan June. I don't want
to leave them
but my life too is a grateful plant
and responds to whatever invitations it receives.

How
does one
achieve
autonomy
when to survive
requires
gratitude? My
lack of it;
that's my secret. How little I feel I owe
anyone.
Anything.

A windy day
and goldfinches in the flowering tree/
how we work our memories to death,
ugly poor old tired old (yes, I know what I am saying)
horses.

I have no memories of Rome,
yet have so absorbed that city from Henry James
it is as if I have fatiguing thoughts there too.

They have gone
the goldfinches
and it was only a minute ago they came
bringing yellow
bringing pleasure
to my mistaken life.

Why the scorn,
brothers,
for ivory? Your towers of flesh
raped,
burned,
destroyed.
　　　　　Human hair grows
for several days
after the body's demise.
　　　　　　　Yet, somehow,
my hair stopped growing
over fifteen years ago.

I read the sad letter of a woman who looks out of her wilderness
　　　　window,
soft white face,
towering
above
mountain
streams. She dreams she sees a
coyote
moving as if ivory had melted, was thick, hard yet flowing,
and silently he stands
listening,
for she is invisible
and he The Trickster, not wearing the cap of darkness,
but instead,
warily,
the white ivory camouflage of visibility.

Who is seen?
Who, the seer?
Love sits alone in her window. Combs her hair.

113

The comb is ivory.
And she is watching a play between beast and man.

Once upon a time, there was Love and she sat in the tower
    window
combing her hair. Death and The Maiden sing the same song.
The Wolf, no, it is a Coyote,
walks quietly in the woods,
the only one sure of
his landscape.

Only, I, the invisible viewer,
look for prints, footprints,
find those
of the King of Spain.

MY MOTHER'S MILKMAN

Cloyce Hamilton,
a slender tan man in white uniform,
with gold teeth,
the truck stopping with foot-clack suddenness
on the gravel road,
the carrier holding four glass bottles of whole milk
with their little paper caps crimped over
the tops.

My mother in her navy blue wool bathrobe
standing by the blue and white tile
kitchen sink, drinking her first morning cup of coffee.

She opens the door for Cloyce
and they stand talking,

for eight years,
three days a week, the Pellissier Dairy Truck
stops with its standing milkman-driver,
Cloyce Hamilton, dressed in white, his tan long wrists and hands
emerging from white starched sleeves,
my mother's King of Spain.

Sometimes my mother ironing in the kitchen
or just drinking her coffee.
Waiting to exchange a few words, or
to catch a glimpse of Cloyce Hamilton or
sometimes
to give him a cup of coffee and listen
to the story of his life.
                         She loved to hear
how a man suffered and longed beyond his milkman's life.

My mother and sister and I
visited the Hamiltons sometimes.
Their house was carpeted, dark, and had
a gold-framed oil painting of a California desert scene
over the mantel.
Vera wore her dark hair in a bun, was handsome,
their house smelled like mothballs and I
envied them; they were typical,
the average American family.
Handsome father who drove his milk truck every day.
Handsome mother who had her dining room table polished and a
         gold-
framed oil over the the mantel.
Two plump girls who wore (and how I envied them)
patent leather shoes.

In my early adolescence
I remembered long murmured conversations between my mother
and Cloyce Hamilton, and then one day
she said we were going to visit Cloyce, that he was no longer
living with Vera and the girls. We went to a tiny house by the
railroad tracks. Inside was the handsome Cloyce and a big teen-
aged boy. I don't remember the boy's name. But Cloyce wanted
to adopt the boy, said my mother, and bring him home, and I
gathered the whispered conversations had been about his struggle
with Vera.

How my mother loved to sympathize with men about their strug-
gles with their wives. My poor, sad, husbandless mother. The
closest she ever came to seduction—listening to the whispers of
angry or frustrated men about their own sad, faithful wives.
Cloyce finally left wife and daughters to live with this tough,
homeless boy.

None of it quite made sense to me.
I questioned and questioned my mother who was a scorpion-
like listener, with her secrets,

dark pools in which undetermined creatures swam.
Now, in retrospect, the story of my mother's milkman
still seems veiled. And sad.
She, such a lonely woman, getting up each morning
for her handsome milkman
who lived the family life she yearned for,
and he, tortured, bent soul
wanting the love of a young boy.

What I remember often is this scene:
    the Hamilton's dark house,
    the gold-framed painting of the California desert
    glowing in the room across from the polished dining room
        table,
    the smell of mothballs,
    the dark Vera, like a Spanish lady,
    and the smell of darkness itself
    in the house.

My mother, believing to the end,
that Cloyce only wanted a son,
never admitting her handsome milkman,
King of Spain,
loved boys.

After all those years of waiting
in the kitchen, at dawn, for the thick milk which she put in her
German coffee.

Drinking.
Fourteen cups a day.
Relieving the black caffein bitterness
with cream from California's
Pellissier Dairy.

Printed February 1980 in Santa Barbara & Ann Arbor for the
Black Sparrow Press by Mackintosh and Young & Edwards
Brothers Inc. Design by Barbara Martin. This edition is
published in paper wrappers; there are 750 hardcover trade
copies; 250 hardcover copies have been numbered & signed by
the author; & 50 numbered copies have been handbound in
boards by Earle Gray each containing an original holograph
poem by Diane Wakoski.

Photo: Robert Turney

Diane Wakoski has published 12 collections of poems, one collection of essays, and many slim volumes of poetry. She serves part of each year as Writer in Residence at Michigan State University.